SYRENA N. WILLIAMS

Living
LIBERATED

Letting Go of the Lies, Labels, and Longing to Be Free

Dedication

If you have ever tried to become the best version of yourself while quietly carrying the weight of your past...

If you have ever smiled in public but wrestled in private...

If you have ever wondered whether freedom was really possible for you...

This book is for you!

God asks each of us to share our testimony so that others may be strengthened. This is mine – offered in faith, so that you may feel loved, seen, and encouraged to live liberated.

SPECIAL ACKNOWLEDGEMENTS

To my son, Syd – you have watched me grow, taught me that parents have so much to learn from their children, and developed your faith as you walked beside me in my journey. You are a major part of my daily desire to live a liberated life.

To my parents, Janice and Fred, thank you for the lessons and the sacrifices that shaped me, even when I was incapable of understanding them at the time.

To my God-designed tribe – the ones God chose for me when I did not know who to choose for myself.

To my publishing team – thank you for your excellence, your patience, and for encouraging me to bring to life what God had planted in me, especially in the details.

And to my future husband, who God is preparing for me, I trust the Author of our story.

With love, courage, and liberation,
Syrena

Contents

Part One: The Lies I Believed

Contents

Introduction

Living Liberated didn't begin with a breakthrough.

It began with a breakdown.

For years, I lived according to a script I didn't write. I performed roles I never auditioned for—dutiful, quiet, responsible, needed, nice. I knew how to deliver. How to show up. How to smile through exhaustion. I was the one others counted on—the fixer, the strong one, the safe place. And because I knew how to function under pressure, I didn't know how to rest in truth.

Underneath the polished surface, I was tired. I had learned to survive. To succeed. To stay silent. But I hadn't learned to be free.

I confused people-pleasing with love. I mistook survival for strength. I wore my pain like it was proof of my purpose. And I lost sight of who I was because I was too busy trying to be who everyone else needed me to be.

I didn't always know I was living in chains.

But once I did, I couldn't unknow it.

This book is the story of what happened when I started telling the truth—first to myself, then to God, then to others. It's about the lies I believed about my worth, my calling, my identity, and my relationships. It's about the labels I wore— smart, cute, strong, successful—but never whole. And it's about the longing I carried to finally feel seen, safe, and free.

You won't find a five-step formula in these pages. This isn't a self-help manual.

It's a mirror. A companion. A healing record.

It holds moments of breakdown in boardrooms, whispers from God in the middle of the night, losses I didn't see coming, and blessings I didn't feel worthy to receive.

It also holds joy. Peace. Laughter. And the sacred invitation to stop striving and start becoming.

If you've ever felt like you had to earn love…

If you've ever wondered if you were too much or not enough…

If you've been silently screaming for something more…

This book is for you.

This is not a story of blame.

It's a story of awakening.

A story of remembering who you were before the world told you who to be.

It's an invitation:

To grieve what you thought you had to become.

To confront what you were never meant to carry.

And to choose a life that's aligned with the truth of who God created you to be.

You don't have to perform anymore.

You don't have to prove anything.

You don't have to wait to be chosen.

You already are.

Now it's time to tell yourself the truth chapter by chapter, lie by lie, one liberating step at a time.

Why I Wrote This Book

I wrote this book because I lived a life that looked successful on the outside but was shaped by lies on the inside. I believed I had to earn love, hide my truth, and settle for whatever was offered — even if it cost me my peace, my purpose, or my dignity. For years, I wore the labels the world gave me and clung to roles that felt familiar, even when they weren't fulfilling. I didn't realize how much those lies were shaping how I showed up — in relationships, in work, and even in faith.

But God wouldn't let me stay stuck. Through tears, therapy, surrender, and scripture, He began peeling back the layers. He showed me that what I had accepted as normal was never His intention for me. He reminded me that my worth isn't determined by my past, my performance, or other people's perception; it's anchored in Him. Slowly, I began to let go of the lies, the labels, and the longing to be chosen. And I began to live free.

This book is my testimony — not of perfection, but of liberation. It's for anyone who has ever felt they had to prove their worth, minimize their brilliance, or stay silent to be accepted. It's for those who have felt stuck between who they used to be and who they're becoming. It's for the person who knows God is calling them higher, but the weight of the past still whispers in their ear.

I want you to know you are not alone. You are not too broken, too late, or too far gone. You were never meant to live bound by shame or fear. You were always meant to live liberated as a beloved child of God, full of purpose, power, and peace.

A Note On Liberation And Love

Jesus said: "Love the Lord your God with all your heart, all your soul, and all your mind." That's the first and greatest commandment. And the second is like it: "Love your neighbor as yourself" *(Matthew 22:37–39)*.

But somewhere along the way, we got the order of the directive wrong.

We tried to love others before learning to love ourselves. And we tried to love ourselves without first learning to receive the love of God.

But here's what I've come to know:

You can't pour from a place that's empty.

You can't reflect a love you've never truly received.

Real love—liberating love—starts with Him.

His love is healing.

His love is truth.

His love sets us free.

When we receive the love of God, we are no longer compelled to prove, perform, or pretend. We're no longer bound by people's opinions or the lies we've carried since childhood. We can walk in peace. We can obey without fear. We can live whole. And we can finally see ourselves the way He does—fearfully and wonderfully made, called, and fully known.

Jesus didn't die so we could live small, scared, and stuck.

He came so we could have life and have it more abundantly *(John 10:10)*.

To live liberated is to love deeply and in the right order:

God first. Then ourselves. Then others.

So this is your reminder, as you walk through these pages:

You were made to be free.

You were made to be loved.

And you were made to love—from the inside out—starting with the God who created you, redeemed you, and calls you by name.

Part One

The Lies I Believed

1

Who Told You That?

I DIDN'T lose my voice all at once. It happened slowly, quietly, in rooms where I learned that confidence could be dangerous and brilliance could be punished. I was a Black girl growing up in America, told early on that I would need to work twice as hard to be seen as half as capable. I heard it in classrooms, from family members, and in the cultural echoes that shaped my identity. That message wasn't always spoken aloud, but it was clear: don't draw too much attention. Don't be too much. Don't be too smart. Don't outshine.

I remember the moment I started hiding. I was in elementary school, age 10. I had always loved school, and I usually knew the answer when the teacher asked a question. I was eager to share my excitement for learning. But after being teased one too many times for "thinking I was smart," my confidence turned into self-protection. I began lowering my hand in middle school at age 12. I stopped answering, even when I knew. Being right had a cost, and that cost was isolation. So I learned to shrink.

The same thing happened with how I looked. I was a light-skinned Black girl, and instead of that being a point of celebration, it became a target. Some kids said I thought I was cute. I never said it, but their insecurities became my burden. To protect myself in high school, I wore baggy clothes to hide my shape. I tried to blend in, while secretly craving the attention I worked so hard to avoid. Because being noticed meant being misunderstood, and being misunderstood meant being left out—or worse.

These weren't just childhood experiences. They became the soil from which my womanhood grew. I became a woman who second-guessed her brilliance. A woman who could light up a room but never fully felt seen in it. A woman who could help everyone else find their voice while struggling to hear her own. I performed with confidence while carrying shame. I gave advice I wasn't sure I believed. I learned how to function through fear. I learned how to disappear in plain sight.

What I didn't know back then was that these messages were lies. They didn't come from God. They came from a world that didn't know how to hold women like me—bold, brilliant, and still becoming. I had begun seeking God intentionally. I was 29 when I read the Bible from beginning to end for the first time. Every year after that, close to my birthday, I paused to evaluate my life. What went well? What didn't? What should I continue, and what needs to change? Each year, I felt the same quiet realization: there was more to life, and somehow, I was missing the mark. One day, as I was deep in my healing journey, I read a familiar biblical passage. The passage is found in Genesis 3:1-11, where God walks through the Garden of Eden after Adam and Eve have eaten the forbidden fruit. They are hiding in shame. And God asks a question that pierced my soul: "Who told you that you were naked?"

I must've read that one line in verse 11 a dozen times, but this time, I saw it differently. God wasn't angry. He was confronting the source of shame. Who told you that? It was less about disobedience and more about deception. God knew they had listened to a voice other than His. And I had too. I had listened to the voice that said I needed to tone myself down. That my value was tied to my usefulness. That silence was safer than the truth.

Those first four words in the question—Who told you that—became a mirror. I began to examine every internalized belief I had been carrying. Who told me I had to earn love? Who told me beauty had to be hidden? Who told me being loud, emotional, or opinionated made me unworthy? Who told me I was too much and not enough at the same time? And why had I spent so many years building my identity around those lies?

> **WE BEGIN TO TREAT GOD LIKE HE AGREES WITH OUR SHAME. BUT HE DOESN'T.**

It's easy to live based on what others have spoken over you, especially if those voices were early, loud, or constant. Parents, teachers, coaches, friends. Their words plant seeds: some that blossom into greatness, others that become weeds of insecurity. And without realizing it, we carry these voices into adulthood, into our relationships, into our faith.

We begin to treat God like He agrees with our shame. But He doesn't.

God never told me to shrink. He never asked me to hide

my intelligence or downplay my gifts. He never called me hard to love. Those were lies. And healing began as I practiced replacing those lies with His words, which are true. I am fearfully and wonderfully made *(Psalm 139:14)*. I am the head and not the tail *(Deuteronomy 28:13)*. I am a masterpiece created in Christ Jesus for good works *(Ephesians 2:10)*. I am His daughter *(1 John 3:1)*.

I am fully seen. Fully loved.

If you've been living under a lie, I want to lovingly interrupt it today. Who told you that you're unworthy? That you'll always be alone? That your voice doesn't matter? That it's too late for you? Was it God, or was it someone who didn't see your value? Someone who was speaking from their own brokenness? It's time to start unlearning. To uproot every false identity. To silence the voices that never came from Him.

This journey isn't about becoming someone new. It's about remembering who you've always been. A daughter. A light. A reflection of God's image. You don't have to earn your worth—it was given. You don't have to apologize for who you are; you were chosen by God. And you don't have to keep living like a *side chick* to the world's approval when you've already been called a King's kid.

So today, ask yourself the same question God asked in the garden: Who told you that? Then pause long enough to hear Him speak the truth back over you.

You are enough.

You are worthy.

You are mine.

2

Never First, Always Second Mentality

BEFORE I ever settled for crumbs in a relationship, I had already been starving in my soul.

I didn't grow up aspiring to be the other woman. That's not how any of this starts. I wanted love, security, and someone who would choose me without hesitation. But somehow, through a slow erosion of self-worth and the repetition of unchecked patterns, I found myself accepting roles, relationships, and realities that didn't honor who I was—or who God said I was becoming.

The thing about the *side chick mentality* is that it doesn't always begin with a relationship. Sometimes it begins with your thoughts, your family history, or the culture that tells you your value lies in your body, your usefulness, or your ability to keep quiet and take what you can get. And over time, that script gets internalized. You stop expecting the fullness of love and settle for emotional leftovers.

I carried a hidden belief that I was disposable. I didn't walk around saying it, but I acted it out by accepting inconsistent communication, conditional affection, and being loved in secret but never in the light. I tolerated being an option because I hadn't yet embraced what it meant to be chosen.

In the world's eyes, I was strong, educated, and accomplished. But behind the scenes, I was negotiating my value with people who were not qualified to affirm me, approve me, or label me. I knew how to speak confidently, but I didn't know how to protect my own heart. I preached boundaries I didn't practice. I called dysfunction loyalty. I labeled pain as passion. I told myself I was in control, but I was really just afraid to be alone.

What I didn't understand then was that the root of my compromise wasn't lust—it was lack. I didn't know who I was, so I kept aligning with people who confirmed my unworthiness. The enemy is not threatened when you choose to be in relationships with people who *say* "God" with their lips but don't *honor* the Savior with their lives. The soul gets tied down in what is said, leading you to become subtly entangled in dishonoring God in your words and practice.

It wasn't about the man or the moment. It was about the lie. The lie that said I had to compete for affection. That I had to over-function to be seen. That I had to earn love with silence and sacrifice. And once those lies took root, it became easier to live beneath the standard God set for me—because it felt familiar.

But God was never confused about my identity. He didn't see me as broken or begging. He saw me as beloved. It took time, scripture, and surrender to unlearn not only what and how I lived, but what I took on from those around me, physically and through the media. I also had to unlearn what the world taught me was normal. I had to study the book of Galatians like my life depended on it—because it did. "You, my brothers and sisters, were called to be free... not to indulge the flesh, but to serve one another humbly in love" *(Galatians 5:13)*.

Freedom didn't feel easy. At first, it felt like loss. Like walking away from what was comfortable. Like sitting in the stillness and not numbing the ache. But each time I chose obedience, each time I returned to the Word, a new identity started to take shape, one that wasn't based on being picked, but on being appointed.

Let me be clear: healing from the side-chick mentality doesn't happen in one sermon or one prayer. I took on this mentality and position in romantic relationships. I was the other woman, the secret girl. But my mind and spirit didn't stay in that quiet acceptance of second place. I was no longer willing to take whatever was offered, especially when someone else held the priority in commitment. A side-chick mentality is secrecy, silencing the Holy Spirit, shrinking standards, staying longer than necessary while pretending to be okay with not being a priority.

At my core, being the other option was the belief that I wasn't worth being fully chosen, and that if I demanded more, I might lose everything. It was shaped by past rejection and fueled by fear, but God never designed me (or you) to compete for priority in love or value.

Healing happens in layers in daily choices. In God encounters that remind you that your worth was never debatable. You already had everything you needed, including worth and value, in Christ.

If you're reading this and parts of your story mirror mine, I want to say this with tenderness and truth:

You are not a side chick! Not in your relationships, your

calling, or your spiritual life. You are not a backup plan.

You are not tolerated.

You are not second in line for God's promises.

You are fully seen. Fully chosen. Fully redeemed.

God doesn't ask you to prove yourself. He simply asks you to believe Him when He says, "You are mine." And when you finally believe it—really believe it—everything begins to change.

3

This Is
All I Knew

I WAS thirteen when my parents separated. I didn't see it coming. One day, my day and my world made sense —even in their imperfections. The next day, everything felt unstable. I was a daddy's girl. I loved him with all my heart. So, when he left, I left. I was confused. I didn't know about his infidelity until he was gone. I didn't understand addiction because I hadn't been exposed to drugs before I was thirteen. I didn't know the signs. All I knew was that the man who said he loved us no longer lived with us, but still came back whenever he wanted to.

As I got older, I became aware that his behavior wasn't

unusual in my environment. Many of my friends' fathers lived the same way. There was often a "main woman" and other women outside of the marriage. All of it was called love. Even my father called it love. He said he was committed to my mother and me, but through his actions, I learned that commitment doesn't necessarily mean consistency. It doesn't mean presence. It doesn't mean faithfulness. Words and actions don't have to match. That became normal for me.

My mother was brilliant, loving, and kind. She tolerated what broke her. That taught me something, too: that strong women sometimes endure what they should end. That love might require accepting what hurts. That stability was flexible.

And here's the lie I believed: inconsistency was normal. That intensity meant love. That if someone chose me for a moment, it was enough. That survival was strength.

When I stepped into my own relationships, I wasn't looking for healthy love. I was looking for familiar. And familiar looked like intensity without security. Promises without proof. Attachment without protection. It was all I knew.

By the time I entered high school, I was already emotionally weary and hungry for stability I was barely fourteen when I entered my first real relationship with a boy my age. It wasn't healthy, but it felt safe in the way familiarity often does. When that relationship fractured, I connected with an older man who made me feel seen and protected. They were vastly different relationships, but both carried emotional and physical depth that I wasn't mature enough to navigate. I stepped into intimacy long before I understood what intimate connections could do to my heart. It felt like love. It felt like being chosen, but it was forming attachments and patterns I wasn't prepared to carry.

One day after school, I had gone to visit my man, when I arrived, I was met by the paramedics carrying his body away. Confused and devastated, I learned that he was a victim of a home invasion. How could this be? He was there one day and murdered the next. This was not my first time experiencing sudden loss; the first was with my father, but it was my first encounter with death.

From that moment on, I stopped expecting things to last. I learned to love temporarily and trust with conditions. My world moved faster than any teenager should have had to run. I learned to play the right roles: the good student, the friend who had it all together, the girl who could make you laugh and then help you strategize your next street move. I lived in duality. I could sit in the classroom and dominate academically and then spend my evenings with people planning drug routes and managing hustle like a business.

Proximity prompted my entry into the world of street narcotics. Proximity to the same kids I had grown up with in classrooms, at bus stops, and on playgrounds. And then, almost overnight, the 1990s crack epidemic reshaped everything. Roles formed quickly. Some became dealers. Some became users. Some became girlfriends, runners, protectors, or enablers. It didn't feel like rebellion. It felt like evolution. Like it was what our world had become.

The drug dealers trusted me with decisions. We had been friends since elementary school. They asked me for counsel. Leaned on me. And in a strange way, I leaned on them too—not for drugs or money, but for a sense of being needed. Even then, my business and leadership mindset were strong. But I was leading in the wrong lane. It gave me a sense of control in a life that had, before then, offered little stability. I was calling the shots in my life now.

I told them not to bring drugs around me. I drew that line early. I told them if I ever got stopped, I'd tell the truth. And they respected it. I thought that was wisdom. But it was really fear masquerading as a boundary. I was trying to keep clean while standing ankle-deep in quicksand.

One night, I attended a party that changed something in me. A turf war had been escalating, and tensions were high. A fight broke out in the middle of the room. A man's throat was cut right in front of me. I was splattered with his blood. One of his crew members grabbed me by the neck, threatening to take my life. But something rose up in me. I looked him dead in the eye and said, "Either kill me or put me down." He dropped me. I walked out. But the trauma clung to me. I was young, but not innocent. I had played a role in an enterprise that destroyed so many.

I was numb.

Somewhere in that chaos, I began seeking God again. The church of my childhood no longer felt like it was meeting the questions rising in me. I was visiting different churches and denominations. I was not searching for God. I was desperate to learn how to pray. My father was battling addiction. His addiction caused my burning desire to learn to pray. My peace was fragile. And my spirit knew there had to be more. I didn't know how to ask for it, but I was reaching. I had no theological depth. I just knew I needed help.

At that point, confusion became my compass. I wasn't moving toward a goal—I was moving away from pain. From being alone. From feeling like I didn't matter. I sought the familiar, even when the familiar was broken. I confused intensity with intimacy. I mistook loyalty for love. I called dysfunction real life. It was all I knew.

I learned how to scan a room, sense danger, and silence my own emotions. I learned how to code-switch, how to adapt, how to make people feel safe, while I was secretly terrified, I didn't have the luxury of emotional breakdowns. I was in performance mode, survival mode, and whatever mode the moment called for.

"

FREEDOM DOESN'T ALWAYS FEEL FAMILIAR. IT OFTEN STARTS WITH DISORIENTATION.

Looking back, I ache for that version of me. She was resilient. She was brilliant. She was carrying more than anyone could see. But she was exhausted. She was becoming numb to things that should have broken her heart. And through it all, God stayed. He didn't walk away. He didn't call me disqualified. He covered me. Whispered to me. Protected me in ways I still can't fully explain.

There's a kind of confusion that comes from contradiction. From being brilliant but broken. From being trusted by others while not trusting yourself. From craving peace but not recognizing it when it shows up. I was living in survival mode, but God was patiently ushering me into something deeper: truth. Identity. Wholeness.

Eventually, I had to confront the reality that just because this was all I knew didn't mean it was all there was. And just because I had learned to function in dysfunction didn't mean God had called me to live there.

Freedom doesn't always feel familiar. It often starts with disorientation. But slowly, I was learning to let God define what normal should be. I was learning that peace doesn't require pain to feel real. And that I didn't have to keep living in confusion just because I knew how to survive it.

4

I Thought It
Was Love

LOVE was the goal. That's what I told myself. I wasn't chasing chaos. I was chasing connection. I didn't set out to lose myself in situationships or soul ties. But when you've been shaped by absence, by inconsistency, by the ache of wanting to be chosen, anything that resembles love, including sex, can feel like the real thing.

I thought it was love when someone made me feel special—even if it was only for a few hours at a time. I thought it was love when someone told me I was beautiful—even if they didn't call the next day. I thought it was love when someone said they needed me—even if they never actually showed up when I needed them. I was living on scraps and calling it a feast. And the lie I had swallowed whole was this: this is as good as it gets for women like me.

I didn't realize then that my definition of love had been shaped by trauma. I was so used to performing, fixing, and absorbing other people's dysfunction that I thought love was something I had to earn. Be quiet enough. Be strong enough. Be useful enough. And maybe, just maybe, you'll be chosen. Not publicly. Not consistently. But chosen enough to silence the doubt—for a moment.

This lie didn't come out of nowhere. It was cultivated by early experiences, by being the fixer, by watching inconsistency get romanticized, by hearing "I love you" used as a cover for control or convenience. And when I looked at my patterns—really looked at them—I realized I was confusing chemistry with clarity. Just because someone made my heart race didn't mean they were sent by God.

There was one relationship I stayed in too long. I gave too much. I believed too deeply in who I thought he could become. He spoke of God, spoke of purpose. But his fruit never matched his words. And every time I mentioned the mismatch, I became the problem. Too emotional. Too demanding. Too spiritual. The gaslighting was subtle—but effective. Over time, I started to question my own discernment.

The truth is, I saw the red flags. But I also saw the potential. I thought my love could inspire him to heal. I thought being loyal would unlock something sacred. I thought sacrifice was a badge of honor. And that's the dangerous part about lies: they don't always show up as darkness. Sometimes they come disguised as light, as good intentions, as "just give it more time." Second Corinthians 11:14 reminds us that even Satan can present himself as an angel of light. Deception rarely announces itself as evil. It often arrives wrapped in a beautiful and sometimes familiar package, presenting itself as spiritual, promising, or full of potential.

What I finally realized was this: I wasn't just fighting for the relationship; I was fighting to prove I was lovable. I wanted the relationship to work so badly because I thought if he chose me, that would mean I was enough. That I was worthy. That the years I had given weren't wasted. But God, in His mercy, let it fall apart. He allowed the illusion to shatter so I could see the truth: I was already loved. And I had been all along.

There's a grief that comes with waking up. It's not just the loss of the relationship; it's the loss of the fantasy. The realization that what you built your hope on was never real. That's where the healing begins. When you can finally say:

this wasn't love. It looked like it. It sounded like it. But it wasn't rooted in truth. And anything not rooted in truth cannot produce fruit that lasts.

God began to teach me a new definition of love. Not just through scripture, but through correction. Through silence. Through redirection. In reading Galatians 5, I realized how much of my behavior had been driven by the flesh, and by the desire to be validated instead of sanctified. God's love doesn't manipulate. It doesn't rush. It doesn't hide. It doesn't cause shame. It shows up to tell the truth. And it heals you without requiring you to lose yourself.

I had to unlearn what I had accepted as normal. Love is not secrecy. It's not pain with a prayer attached. It's not potential that never manifests. Love, real love, is sacrificial, yes—but it's mutual. It's whole. And it always points you back to the One who loved you first.

The lie was that I had to prove I was lovable. The truth is, I was already chosen by a God who never changes His mind. And when you start from that truth, you stop chasing validation and start walking in purpose. You stop settling for emotional breadcrumbs and start preparing for the feast that's been waiting on you all along.

5

I Stayed
Too Long

THERE'S a moment in every unhealthy relationship where you know it's time to go. Then, there's the moment you actually leave. For me, those moments were often years apart. I didn't stay because I was stupid. I stayed because I was scared. I stayed because I had hope. I stayed because I believed the lie that said enduring mistreatment was a sign of strength and loyalty.

Leaving is hard when you've made someone your project. You keep waiting for the turnaround. You pray for the moment they'll finally get it. You think your patience will be rewarded. But what often happens instead is that your delay becomes your undoing. The longer I stayed, the more I lost sight of myself. My voice got quieter. My standards got lower. And my pain got louder.

It's easy to convince yourself that your story will be the exception. This time, your love will be enough to change someone. This time, if you pray harder, forgive faster, and serve more faithfully, it'll all work out. And when it doesn't, you don't just grieve the person. You grieve the future you were building in your head. You grieve the version of yourself that thought you could carry it all.

In my thirties, I became a side-chick again, but this time with a married man. After 10 years of grappling with myself, I knew I had outgrown this relationship. Marriage was never going to happen between us. It wasn't abusive. It was just spiritually and emotionally misaligned. I had grown in my faith and purpose, and he hadn't. We weren't walking in the same direction anymore. But I was afraid of the disruption. Afraid of having to explain. Afraid of starting over. So, I stayed. I made excuses. I played small. I gave what I didn't have. And I kept calling it love.

But real love doesn't make you shrink. It doesn't make you question your sanity. It doesn't require you to betray your own values to maintain peace. The longer I stayed, the more I realized I wasn't being loyal—I was being afraid. I was afraid no one else would want me. Afraid that I was asking for too much. Afraid that God might not come through if I let go.

One of the lies I believed was that endurance equals faithfulness. But not all endurance is holy. Sometimes endurance is fear in disguise. God never asked me to stay in a space where my purpose had been suffocated. He never called me to be anyone's savior. That role was already taken.

> **LOVE IS NOT PROVEN BY HOW LONG YOU SUFFER. IT'S PROVEN BY HOW WELL YOU STEWARD YOUR SOUL.**

When I finally left, it wasn't with fanfare or applause. It was quiet. Grieving. Humbling. But it was right. And on the other side of that decision, I found peace. Things were not perfect, but I was no longer betraying myself in the name of love.

Staying too long cost me years. It cost me clarity. But it also taught me something priceless: love is not proven by how long you suffer. It's proven by how well you steward your soul.

God calls us to be good stewards *(1 Corinthians 4:2)*.

Stewardship is not only about money. It's about everything He has entrusted to us: our time, our bodies, our gifts, our children, our influence, and yes, even our souls. Our peace. Our identity. Our emotional and spiritual health. These are not disposable; they are divine deposits from God into the fabric of our creation.

To steward your soul means you guard what God placed inside you. You protect your clarity. You honor your convictions. You refuse to participate in relationships that require you to abandon your obedience to God to maintain connection with someone else. You live as if every part of you is on loan from heaven, because it is.

And if someone requires you to lose yourself to love them, it's not love. It's bondage.

I used to think that God wanted me to hold on at all costs. But what He really wanted was my freedom. My healing. My obedience. And sometimes, obedience looks like walking away—not because you're bitter, but because you're finally becoming whole.

Leaving doesn't mean you failed. It means you woke up. And there is grace for the years you stayed. Grace for the confusion. Grace for the healing process. And most of all, grace to begin again—this time, with your dignity intact and your identity secure.

6

I Am My Own Enemy

SOME battles don't come from outside of us. They rage within. And the hardest truth I had to face was this: no one sabotaged me more consistently than I had.

It's a difficult confession to make, especially when you've lived through real betrayal, real pain, real abandonment. But once I started unpacking the patterns—missed opportunities, unfinished projects, relationships I knew better than to entertain—I saw the common denominator. Me.

I blamed other people for a long time.

For not seeing my worth. For wasting my time. For treating me like an option. And yes, some of that was real. But the deeper truth was that I had allowed it. I had made myself small. I had lowered the bar. I stayed silent when I should have spoken. And I called it humility. I called it submission. I even called it faith. But it was fear. It was insecurity. It was self-sabotage—like dressing a wound instead of treating the infection underneath.

There were dreams I had that never got off the ground; not because they weren't valid, but because I was waiting for perfect conditions. Waiting for certainty. Waiting for someone else to believe in me more than I believed in myself. I delayed progress in the name of preparation, but deep down, I was terrified of failing publicly. Or worse—succeeding and not knowing how to handle it.

One of the lies I believed was that I wasn't ready. That I needed more time, more affirmation, more confirmation. I ignored the fact that I had prayed, studied, and prepared. I was anointed, but still afraid. And that fear dressed itself up in procrastination, perfectionism, and imposter syndrome.

I was the kind of woman who could hype up everyone else. I could see greatness in others from a mile away. But when it came to me? I questioned everything. I minimized my own voice. I downplayed my own brilliance. And I called it modesty. But God never asked me to be invisible. He asked me to be obedient.

Obedience is listening to Him daily in the quiet and doing exactly what He said without negotiating, delaying, or diluting His directives. For me, it was simple things: call this person, give this to that person, encourage her, help him. Small instructions that required sensitivity to the Holy Spirit and trust. But obedience has a way of stretching you. The whispers became weightier: speak up in that room, say these exact words in that room, launch the business, stop hiding behind other people's visions, end those relationships that are draining your oil.

I had been faithfully serving everyone else's assignment while sidelining my own. I found ways to justify it because it looked noble. I was supporting. I was helping. I was being a "servant leader." But underneath that service was fear of becoming more, fear of being seen, fear of stepping fully into what God designed me to carry. Playing in the background felt safer than risking expansion.

The moment I realized I was the one standing in my own way, everything shifted Not because the fear disappeared, but because I finally understood that immediately doing what God said was not optional. God wasn't waiting for me to feel confident. He was waiting for me to trust Him enough to move and to change. The real sabotage was my hesitation in saying yes consistently when God spoke.

God doesn't wait for us to feel worthy to use us. He waits for us to say yes. And when I started saying yes before I had all the answers, before I felt confident, before I knew how it would end, He met me there. He multiplied my yes. He refined me along the way.

If you've been stuck in a cycle of false starts and internal sabotage, I get it. But here's what I know now: God is not intimidated by your hesitation. He wants your heart. He wants your surrender. And He wants you to stop shrinking from the very thing He put in you.

The lie was that I wasn't ready. The truth is that God equips those He calls—and He called me. He called you. And the moment you stop fighting yourself, you'll discover how much ground you can actually take. Not because of perfection. But because of obedience.

I am no longer my own enemy.

I am my advocate. My encourager. My partner with God. And that shift didn't happen overnight. But it started with one decision: to believe what God said about me more than the doubts screaming inside my head.

7

I Thought I Had
To Do It All

I USED to believe that asking for help was a sign of weakness. That strong women don't complain, don't collapse, and certainly don't confess when they're overwhelmed. I thought strength meant doing it all, handling it all, fixing it all. Alone.

That lie was so deeply embedded in me that I didn't even recognize it as a lie. I wore my exhaustion like a badge of honor. I thought that being tired all the time meant I was doing something right. That always being needed meant I was valuable. That holding everyone else together was my purpose.

But the truth is, I was secretly leading, managing, caring, producing, providing, and drowning. Every day felt like a performance I didn't audition for. I was the solution for everyone else's problems, but I had nowhere to lay my own. I didn't know how to rest. I didn't know how to let go. I didn't know how to say, "I can't do this."

And then it all caught up with me. I found myself curled up in a ball on the floor next to my bed every night. I was too tired to think, and too overwhelmed to cry. I was taking care of my father, my child, my partner, my law firm, and my own failing health. But no one knew how bad it had gotten because I didn't let them see it. I didn't want to see it myself.

It took two voices to wake me up. One was my partner's, who looked at me one night and said, "You're going to die taking care of someone who doesn't care about you." The other voice came through a girlfriend who asked me a question that shook me to my core. "When did God ask for your help?"

That question haunted me in the best way. Because it forced me to confront a truth I had been avoiding. I had taken on burdens God never asked me to carry. I had stepped into roles He never assigned me. I was playing savior instead of being obedient. I was over-functioning in the name of love, loyalty, and legacy—and it was killing me.

I believed that being responsible meant being indispensable. But God never called me to do it all. He called me to trust Him. To rest in Him. To walk in wisdom, not martyrdom.

I began learning to delegate tasks and emotional weight. I began saying no without apology. I began letting people sit in their own consequences instead of rescuing them. And most of all, I began asking for help. From God. From friends. From professionals. I stopped spiritualizing burnout and started honoring my own humanity.

Jesus didn't do it all. Even He delegated. Even He got away to rest. Even He had boundaries. And if the Son of God didn't try to carry the weight of the world alone, why did I think I had to?

Letting go wasn't easy. It felt like failure at first. But slowly, it began to feel like freedom. I realized that being everything to everyone was never sustainable—and it was never my assignment.

The truth is, I don't have to do it all. I just have to do what God asked me to do. And when I stay in my lane, there's grace there. There's peace. There's clarity. And there's room for others to rise and serve, too.

Surrender isn't a sign of weakness—it's the beginning of

wellness. And I am no longer afraid to ask for help, to rest, or to say, "that's not mine to carry." I am no longer proving my worth through my exhaustion. I am receiving my worth from the One who already called me worthy—without me lifting a finger.

Part Two

The Wake-Up Call

8

I Thought I Was
The Exception

SOMEWHERE along the way, I convinced myself that the rules didn't fully apply to me. Not in an arrogant way, at least, that's what I told myself. It was more subtle than that. I thought I could outrun consequences. That since I had good intentions and a sincere heart, God would give me a pass on what He required from others.

I saw the warnings. I felt the red flags. I knew when the Holy Spirit was whispering, "Not this. Not now. Not them." But I overrode it. I prayed while still negotiating. I fasted while still holding on. I tithed while justifying my disobedience. And I told myself, "God understands my heart." I thought that understanding would translate into exemption.

The truth is, I thought I could love people enough to make it work. Collaborate with people who weren't aligned. Partner in business with those whose character didn't match their confession. I let God talk fool me. I heard the right phrases—"favor," "faith," "kingdom"—and I assumed that meant covering. But in reality, I was being seduced by potential and ignoring the evidence of fruit.

I said yes to a collaborative project because it looked promising. On paper, it was a divine opportunity—shared work, shared income, shared impact. But underneath, the foundation was cracked. There was pride where there should have been humility. Control where there should have been trust. I ignored the early signs. I didn't pray before I committed. I just moved. Fast. And I believed the lie that I could fix it on the way.

"

ANOINTING DOESN'T CANCEL ACCOUNTABILITY.

When pressure hit, so did the truth. The same people who spoke God's name in public were cursing and backbiting in private. Meetings turned hostile. Trust disintegrated. I found myself in rooms where I no longer recognized the spirit of the work. What started as a collaboration turned into spiritual contamination. And I couldn't pray my way out of what I had never asked God to lead me into.

That was my wake-up call: I am not the exception to obedience. I don't get to bypass discernment. I don't get to partner without prayer. I don't get to excuse red flags and then blame God for the fallout. And just because something has potential doesn't mean it's purposeful for me.

There's a difference between grace and approval. God had graced me to endure—but He had not approved my decision. He covered me, but I still had to clean up the consequences. I still had to sit in the discomfort of knowing that I had opened a door He never asked me to walk through.

One of the most sobering truths I've learned is this: anointing doesn't cancel accountability. I don't get a pass because I'm gifted. I don't get divine protection from the outcomes of decisions I make without Him. I am not the exception. And that realization, while painful, saved me.

It taught me to pause. To pray first. To listen for alignment—not just language. To trust fruit over familiarity. To walk away from opportunities that don't carry His peace. And to remember that just because I can doesn't mean I should.

I no longer live under the illusion that God will bless every door I knock on. Now, I ask Him to close what's not from Him before I walk through, and then I must be rescued from what looked good but wasn't God.

The lie was that I could bend divine instructions to fit my desire. The truth is that obedience is not optional—and I am not the exception. But thankfully, God is faithful. Even when I move too fast, He waits. Even when I ignore the signs, He sends confirmation. And even when I step outside of His will, He calls me back—not with condemnation, but with clarity.

I thought I was the exception. But now I know—I'm the called. And that comes with a weight of responsibility I can no longer pretend doesn't exist.

9

The Boardroom Breakdown

THERE'S a certain kind of breakdown that doesn't happen at home, in private, with the blinds drawn. It happens under fluorescent lights, in tailored clothes, with your laptop open and a leadership title hanging over your head. That's where mine happened—in a boardroom.

I was juggling it all. Running a firm, managing people, showing up in every room like I had it all together. I had trained myself to be calm under pressure, articulate in crisis, strategic in storms. But that day, something broke. It wasn't loud. It wasn't public. But it was seismic. Something in me collapsed, and I couldn't hold it up anymore.

It didn't start as a breakdown. It started as a moment of disconnect. I was in a meeting, surrounded by people who were smart and capable, but the conversation felt foreign. I had done the prep, I knew the data, but I couldn't focus. My mind was racing and blank at the same time. I was nodding, smiling, adding bullet points—and dying inside.

The night before, I had been crying alone in my car. Again. The kind of cry that's silent but shaking. The kind where you grip the steering wheel, not to drive, but just to hold on to something. And that morning, I had straightened my hair, put on my confidence, and walked into that room like I hadn't just been unraveling twelve hours earlier.

But in that moment, I felt God speak—not with thunder, but with clarity. I heard: "This is not where your wholeness lives." It wasn't about the people, the room, or the work. It was about me. I had wrapped my identity so tightly around what I could produce that I had stopped paying attention to what I was becoming.

The lie I believed was that success would make the struggle worth it. That if I could just keep climbing, just keep proving, just keep pushing—I would finally feel whole. But what I learned in that boardroom was this: no title can heal a wounded identity. No amount of recognition can fill a soul that still feels unseen.

After that meeting, I excused myself and walked to the restroom. I looked at myself in the mirror and didn't recognize the woman staring back. Not because I looked different, but because I had become a stranger to my own truth. I had been performing for so long that I had started to believe the role. But the real me? She was tired. She was grieving. She was ready to stop pretending.

That breakdown was a beginning. It was the moment I stopped spiritualizing burnout. The moment I stopped connecting my worth to my work. The moment I realized that overachievement is just a dressed-up form of fear. And it was the moment I decided I didn't want to keep living like that—not for another meeting, not for another deal, not for another round of applause.

God never asked me to sacrifice myself on the altar of success. He called me to steward my gifts, yes—but not at the cost of my soul. That boardroom breakdown was holy. It was the end of a chapter I had been afraid to close. And the start of deeper healing that I didn't know I needed.

I no longer see breakdowns as failures. I see them as divine interventions. God will sometimes let what you built in your own strength collapse just to show you what He can build when you surrender. That day, I didn't lose anything. I found something: truth. And it set me free.

10

When Did God Ask For Your Help?

I'VE ALWAYS been someone who steps up. If something needed fixing, I was already on it. If someone needed support, I was the shoulder they could lean on. If there was a gap, I filled it. No questions asked. I wore my reliability like a uniform and called it purpose. But somewhere in the swirl of all my doing, I crossed a line I couldn't see; I started carrying things God never asked me to pick up.

It was a season that should've taken me out. My law firm needed attention. My father's health was declining. My child needed guidance. My partner needed care. And in the middle of all that, my own health was deteriorating. I developed a hyperthyroid condition that prevented me from sleeping. I managed to keep it together in public, but every night, once home, I collapsed and could only sleep for a few hours. I was quietly unraveling. Because I thought that's what strong women do.

The exhaustion wasn't just emotional; it was also physical. The Black Lives Matter Movement emerged during my child's college years, adding another layer of emotional weight and vigilance. And still, I kept going.

I gave everything to my father – every appointment, every advocacy call, every ounce of effort – desperately trying to provide what he needed, even when he refused to care for himself. It was a daily fight, a season marked by resistance and disrespect. He didn't receive my care lovingly. I was risking my health, my peace, and my stability without acknowledgement of my sacrifice, efforts, or love.

My wakeup call came as I was catching up with my friend over lunch. We were sharing what was happening in our lives, and I was crying from exhaustion over what my life was filled with. Calmly, she looked at me with concern and said in a kind tone, "When did God ask for your help?"

I felt a jolt in my spirit because I had heard similar words from a previous partner, "You're going to die taking care of someone that doesn't care about you."

Those conversations really woke me up. I was forced to examine my motives and capacity to keep going. To this day, whenever I find myself taking on too much, I can hear their voices reminding me to release what is not mine to carry. I ask myself, am I doing what God asked, or am I doing what might make me look needed and feel valuable?

I had a habit of taking on battles that weren't mine. Tried to orchestrate outcomes I couldn't control. I had mistaken busyness for calling. Movement for faithfulness. I had inserted myself into places where God never assigned me—and then wondered why I was drowning.

Those questions became a mirror. And what I saw in myself was a woman who believed the lie that being helpful was the same as being virtuous. That God needed me to get it done. That exhaustion was just part of the assignment. But that's not the God I serve. He doesn't reward burnout. He doesn't require martyrdom. He doesn't call us to be saviors—He already did that.

I had to admit something even deeper and more convicting: I didn't trust God to handle what I couldn't control.

Since then, I've started asking different questions. Not "Can I do this?" "Is this mine to do?" Not, "How do I keep everything together?" But "What has God actually asked me to carry?" And I've learned that discernment is just as spiritual as service. Wisdom is just as sacred as sacrifice.

I now measure faithfulness not by how much I do but by how much I obey. And if God doesn't ask for my help, I don't volunteer for the burden. Because obedience is lighter. Grace is sufficient. And surrender doesn't mean giving up. It means letting God be God and letting myself be human. Surrender means living by a new truth: I am not the answer. He is.

11

They Paid Me
To Leave

THERE are moments when God allows discomfort to become undeniable—not as punishment, but as preparation. I was working in my first Human Resources management position, newly out of college. A job that, on the outside, looked ideal. The title was respectable. The work was meaningful. The pay was steady. Then came the soul-tug moment many feel on their career ride: a good title and consistent income were not fulfilling. I was suffocating.

At first, I tried to brush it off. Everyone gets tired, right? Everyone feels stuck sometimes. I told myself to push through. But the pressure kept building. I wasn't only tired—I was depleted. Spiritually, emotionally, physically. The tipping point came when my boss asked me to falsify documents ahead of an audit.

I wish I could say I was surprised, but the truth is, the culture had been corroding for a while. Integrity was optional. Image was everything. And even though I knew who I was—and more importantly, whose I was—there was still a moment of hesitation. That's what scared me the most. Not that he asked, but that part of me considered it for the sake of peace and security.

That moment forced me to choose: my character or my comfort. I chose to walk. Quietly. Resolutely. No fanfare. No fiery email. Just a resignation that said: I won't be a part of this.

What happened next still feels surreal. They called me back. Not because they had changed their minds, but because no one else knew how to do what I did. They needed me to come back and teach them the very systems they had ignored when I was employed. And this time? They paid me four times the rate.

I didn't gloat. I didn't puff up. I showed up, did the work, and walked away. But deep inside, something shifted. And in that moment, God made it clear: you never lose when you obey Me. What looks like loss to others is often deliverance in disguise. What feels like being dismissed is sometimes divine redirection.

The lie I had believed was that leaving meant failure. That walking away meant I wasn't strong enough to handle it. But the truth is, staying would have been the real failure. Staying would've meant betraying my values. Staying would've meant forfeiting the peace I had fought so hard to protect.

Sometimes God will let a door close so obviously that you can't pretend it's still your assignment. And when you walk away with clean hands and a clear heart, He often provides in ways that make it undeniable: this was Him. Not luck. Not a coincidence. Him.

Being paid more to leave than I ever made while staying was not just poetic—it was prophetic. It reminded me that provision doesn't come from people. It comes from God. And when I trust Him enough to walk away from what's misaligned, I make room for what's divine.

Now, I no longer ask, "What if they need me?" I ask, "Is this where God called me to be?" Because the truth is, sometimes your greatest breakthrough is on the other side of your boundary. And yes, they paid me to leave, but

I gained more than a check. I gained clarity. I gained confidence. I gained freedom.

Leaving was not the end. It was the invitation to begin again—this time, with my peace intact and my purpose reawakened.

12

The Pattern Breaker

THERE comes a moment in every healing journey when you realize: someone must go first. Someone must stop the cycle, break the agreement, choose differently. For me, that moment came not with a loud declaration, but with a quiet decision—I would be the pattern breaker.

> **BREAKING PATTERNS DOESN'T START WITH REBELLION. IT STARTS WITH AWARENESS.**

Breaking patterns doesn't start with rebellion. It starts

with awareness. It's waking up one day and realizing that just because something has always been done a certain way doesn't mean it's the way God intends for it to continue moving forward. It's recognizing the silent agreements passed down like heirlooms: that women must carry everything, that survival is success, that love requires suffering, that silence equals strength.

I had inherited these lies without even realizing it. They weren't always taught, but they were quietly modeled. In whispered phone calls, in tired eyes, in family secrets. They showed up in how we navigated money, conflict, grief, and even faith. And for a long time, I thought I was just doing what had to be done. But what I was really doing was repeating what had never been healed.

God began to reveal the patterns. He did so with mercy and grace. The revelations never brought shame, only conviction and reassurance that He wanted me to surrender to the transformation He was performing. I started seeing how my decisions, what I said yes to, what I tolerated, and what I hid were tied to old wounds and outdated beliefs. I wasn't just living my life; I was reliving someone else's fear, someone else's silence, someone else's script.

Becoming a pattern breaker required more than awareness—it required courage. Courage to say no. Courage to rest. Courage to raise my voice. Courage to be misunderstood and not let it shrink me. Courage to choose obedience to God over tradition. And the courage to trust that the cost of breaking the pattern was still less than the cost of passing it down.

There were moments when I felt alone. Like no one understood the fight I was in. But God reminded me: I was not just doing this for myself. I was doing it for my child, for my lineage, for the women watching me, and for the version of myself who didn't know this kind of freedom was possible.

I stopped explaining my obedience to people who benefited from my silence. I started walking away from spaces that required me to abandon myself to belong. I started believing that God didn't just want me healed; He wanted me whole. Not just functional, but free.

The lie I believed was that change would cost me everything. The truth is, it gave me back what mattered most: peace, clarity, integrity, and alignment with God. And the fruit of that obedience is visible—not just in me, but in every person now free to make a different choice because I did.

Being the pattern breaker doesn't mean I have it all figured out. It means I'm no longer pretending the pattern isn't there. It means I'm letting the Holy Spirit rewrite the scripts I used to live by and wrote on my own. It means I'm choosing legacy over loyalty to dysfunction. And it means I'm finally walking in the authority that was always mine — but could only be unlocked by obedience.

I am not the fixer. I am not the savior. I am the one who said yes to healing. Yes, to truth. Yes, to freedom. And by God's grace, my yes is making room for others to say yes too. That is what it means to be the pattern breaker. And I wouldn't trade it for anything.

Part Three

Living Liberated

13

I Found
My Rhythm

LIVING liberated doesn't mean living perfectly. It means living with intention, alignment, and grace. I used to think that wholeness looked like having everything figured out. That living liberated meant balance, structure, and getting it all done. But I've learned that liberation feels more like rhythm—moving with God rather than ahead of Him.

For years, I wore busyness like a badge of honor. My calendar was packed, my phone never stopped buzzing, and my body stayed in motion. I confused productivity with purpose and exhaustion with excellence. If I was tired, I believed I must be doing something right. But what I was really doing was running from silence, because silence required honesty. And honesty would have revealed that I was out of alignment.

I first began noticing the signs when I felt perpetually irritable. Little things got under my skin. I was snappy, short-fused, and emotionally raw. My mornings started with pressure, and my nights ended in depletion. Even the things I loved—serving, leading, and creating—started to feel heavy. That's when I knew: I wasn't more than tired. I was misaligned.

God doesn't create in chaos. He creates in rhythm. From the beginning, He set the world into motion with cadence—light and dark, work and rest, seedtime and harvest. And yet, I had built a life on constant output. There was no space for breath, for reflection, for Him. And He gently showed me: this wasn't the abundant life He promised. This was just a high-functioning version of burnout. A routine of misalignment that I continued to ask God to give me strength for, but it never came.

Finding my rhythm came through a series of surrendered moments. It was learning to say no to good things to protect the God things. It was practicing Sabbath—not as a reward for working hard, but as a declaration that I trust God more than I trust my hustle. It was letting peace—not pressure—determine my pace.

I started noticing the patterns in my body. When I'm out of rhythm, I don't sleep well. I crave sugar. I forget to drink water. My shoulders stay tense. My joy feels brittle. So now, when I feel those cues, I pause. I reassess. I ask God: Where did I get off track? What did I take on that wasn't mine?

One of the most freeing truths I've embraced is that peace is a compass. If I have to force it, beg for it, or rush it—it's probably not for me. That applies to work, ministry, relationships, and opportunities. God's rhythm always comes with peace, even when it requires effort.

> **IS THIS MINE TO CARRY RIGHT NOW?**

Now, I live by rhythm. I rise early, not to chase productivity, but because I crave stillness. I pause during my day to breathe, to pray, to listen. I create margin. I protect rest. I embrace joy. And when I slip into striving, I don't shame myself; I simply return. Rhythm is less about rules and more about remembering who sets the pace.

I've learned to stop asking, "Can I do it all?" Instead, I ask, "Is this mine to carry right now?" Because when I move with God, things flow. When I don't, things fracture. And the more I trust His timing, the more liberated I become.

Liberation isn't found in the hustle. It's found in the rhythm of obedience, grace, and rest. It's found in opening your heart, mind, and soul to His voice. And in that rhythm, I've found something I was missing for years: sustainable peace, sacred stillness, and the joy of living at the speed of God.

14

He Changed
My Name

THERE are movements that feel small on the surface but shift everything underneath. A phone call. A question. A pause. For me, it came when I was in the middle of transitioning out of a professional partnership. I had done everything right, documented the buyout terms, submitted the necessary paperwork, and followed the guidelines. But the governing agency didn't approve it. They called to tell me I could not keep the firm's name.

I tried to maintain my composure, even as tears silently fell down my face. I had built that firm with my own hands. I sacrificed and served. And now I was being told I couldn't carry the name forward. I prepared to end the call politely, but before I could hang up, the agent said something I'll never forget: "Ms. Williams, what's wrong with your name?"

This question echoed deeper than business Scripture says, "A good name is to be chosen rather than great riches" *(Proverbs 22:1)*. I had been grieving the loss of a brand while overlooking the inheritance already attached to my own name. My name was and is not a liability; it is a legacy.

Right there, in the middle of my grief and frustration, God used an unexpected messenger to remind me: your name is enough. You are enough. And I am not hiding you anymore.

That question wasn't just administrative—it was divine. It was the moment I stopped asking for permission to exist. I began living liberated—no longer confined by others' terms. I hung up the phone and decided that day: I would no longer attach my future to what someone else started. I would build from my own foundation, with the name God gave me. I launched Syrena Williams Legal Services—and something in me shifted.

I realized that God wasn't just calling me to serve clients—He was calling me to stand. To be seen. To carry His light with confident compassion. He had covered me in seasons of partnership, but now He was asking me to step out fully, boldly, and visibly. I wasn't just representing a business. I was representing a kingdom identity.

Since that day, I've become the face of not just my law firm, but of my coaching and consulting work as well. My name is now tied to every room I enter. And while that used to terrify me, now it grounds me. It reminds me that I'm accountable—not just to my goals, but more importantly, to God. Not just to my reputation, but to my purpose.

I started asking different questions: What would make God smile? What message am I sending by how I show up? What's the footprint I'm leaving behind? Whether I'm speaking, writing, coaching, or filing legal documents, am I doing it from a place of authenticity, humility, and excellence?

When God changes your name, He changes your assignment. He reorients your posture from shrinking to standing tall, from playing small to living liberated. He gives you visibility not for your ego, but for His glory. And what felt like a loss—no longer being able to keep the firm's name—was a sacred invitation to come out of hiding.

Just like He changed Abram to Abraham, Sarai to Sarah, and Jacob to Israel—God gave me a name to walk in the fullness of my purpose.

There's nothing wrong with your name when God's hand is on it. My name has become the banner I live under, not out of pride, but out of liberation. And now, I wear that name with honor. Not because I'm flawless. But because I'm called. I'm chosen. And I'm committed to showing up fully as who He created me to be—by name, by grace, and by design.

The Bible tells us that a good name is more valuable than silver or gold. God is still establishing names today. He is still calling people from their hiding places. He is still placing His weight and His glory on ordinary people and making them vessels of extraordinary purpose. When His hand rests on your life, it carries authority that money cannot buy and favor that no partnership can manufacture.

15

Motherhood Made
Me Mindful
(And Free)

MOTHERHOOD has been my greatest classroom. It's the role that taught me how much I didn't know, how deeply I could love, and how urgently I needed God. I didn't enter motherhood with a full understanding of faith. I believed in God, but I wasn't in a relationship with Him. I knew how to pray, but I hadn't yet learned how to surrender, seek, and find. And yet, from the moment I became a mother, I knew I had to live differently—because someone was watching me to learn how to live. And slowly, motherhood became the first place I practiced living liberated—imperfectly so, but present. Incomplete, but available to God.

When Syd was young, I tried to be everything: present, responsible, disciplined, loving. I took motherhood seriously, in practice and intention. My schedule, my money, and my mindset had to shift. But what shifted most over time was my awareness. I became mindful of how I moved, how I reacted, and what I modeled. I realized that the way I lived would shape what Syd believed about God, love, responsibility, and identity.

I grew up in a large family where words were unfiltered. If someone thought it, they said it. Direct. Sharp. Sometimes carelessly. My mother was loving and kind most of the time, but her wit could cut. I learned early how powerful words could be and how they could build and bruise in the same breath. And I made a quiet decision to keep the warmth, but surrender the sharpness. I would not let my tongue become a weapon camouflaged as honesty. I was mothering with memories that shaped me.

My mother was warmth but, in some ways, naïve. There were parts of my teenage life she never saw. Things she didn't know. I carried that awareness into my own parenting with urgency. I didn't want Syd living a life I wasn't aware of. I didn't want distance masked as independence. But I didn't know how to build full trust without control. I didn't know how to invite honesty without it sounding like judgment.

I was opinionated. Strong. Clear about what I believed, and sometimes that strength felt like scrutiny to him. Motherhood began teaching me restraint. It taught me that not every thought required my voice. That listening could be more powerful than lecturing. That presence wasn't the same as pressure. And slowly, God used my child to soften me in ways I didn't know I needed.

But even with all that care and intention, there was still that lingering fear every parent carries: Did I do enough? Did I leave a godly impression? Would my child seek God when it mattered?

That question followed me quietly—until one night, while Syd was in college. The country was in turmoil over police brutality and the murder of George Floyd. Racial tensions were high. Fear and confusion spread across campus, and the students were scared. Some made threats. Others huddled together, unsure of what to do, as Black Lives Matter became the defining social justice movement of their generation.

Syd called me. Not for advice. Not to vent. But to ask for one thing: "Mom, I'm going to put you on speaker. Can you please pray?"

In that moment, I knew. The seed had been planted. God had not only watered it in me, but He was also watering it in my child. Syd didn't run to fear or anger. Syd ran to faith. Somewhere along the way, through all my stumbles and growth, I had made prayer visible. I had made seeking God normal. And it took root.

That call humbled me. It reminded me that mindful motherhood isn't about control; it's about presence. It's about being faithful with what you know and letting God cover the rest. It's about leading while still learning. Teaching while still being transformed. And most of all, it's about trusting that what you plant in love and faith will bloom— maybe not on your timeline, but always in God's.

Motherhood made me mindful because it made me accountable. I realized that my choices had ripple effects beyond me. That my healing mattered not just for me, but for the child watching me become whole. And now, even as Syd walks his own journey, I still feel that sacred call to model surrender, faith, and grace.

You don't have to have all the answers to be a good mother. You only need to be present, prayerful, and willing to grow. Liberation begins in the honesty of your effort and the grace of God's covering. The rest, God handles. And in that way, motherhood didn't just grow a child—it grew me. It freed me. And continues to liberate me.

16

I Hear God Clearly

I USED to think that hearing from God was reserved for pastors, prophets, and deeply spiritual people. That, unless I was kneeling at an altar or fasting for forty days, I couldn't expect to receive clear direction. But over time, I learned that God doesn't need theatrics. He needs access. He speaks to the ones who make room to listen. And when we do, we start to live liberated—no longer bound by confusion, striving, or needing someone else to tell us what God already placed in our hearts.

God has been speaking to me my entire life. Sometimes in ways I understood. Often in ways I didn't. But when I started making space for Him—intentional, uninterrupted space—He began meeting me at the appointed time. Early in the morning, before the world could speak louder than His whisper, He started waking me.

At first, I resisted. I told myself I was too tired. I justified sleeping in. But God didn't let me sleep through the night. Every time I ignored the prompt, I'd wake up restless. Wide-eyed at 3 a.m. with a stirring in my spirit. When I finally said yes, when I stopped resisting, and started rising, He met me. Daily. Faithfully. And the more I honored His invitation, the more clearly I began to hear.

One of the ways God speaks to me is through short, simple phrases. Rarely a full sentence. Just a word or two—enough to lead me into prayer, meditation, and eventually, revelation. Years ago, He gave me a phrase: "The One." No context. No instructions. Just those two words. And I wrote them down. I prayed. I waited. I asked for clarity. I assumed it was a message for someone else. I shared it with a few trusted voices, but none of them felt assigned to it. So I held it, and I listened.

Time passed. Then one day, I heard another directive: "Call Olalah." We hadn't spoken in five years. We had only met in person once. But I had learned not to let awkwardness delay obedience. I called. And that one act of obedience unlocked a divine partnership. One year later, we hosted the first The One Experience and launched a nonprofit built on the foundation of light, faith, and transformation.

That's how God moves in my life. A whisper. A name. A nudge. And then, if I'm willing to respond, a revelation. Not all at once. But always right on time.

I no longer question whether it's God or my own thoughts. Not because I'm always certain in the moment, but because I've learned that peace confirms the prompting. When God speaks, there is a knowing. A steadiness. A quiet urgency that aligns with Scripture, character, and purpose. And when I obey, even if it doesn't make sense at first, the fruit always follows.

> **HEARING GOD CLEARLY ISN'T ABOUT BEING PERFECT. IT'S ABOUT BEING POSITIONED.**

Hearing God clearly isn't about being perfect. It's about being positioned. It's about choosing stillness over striving. It's about expecting Him to speak and refusing to treat His voice like background noise. Whether it's through Scripture, prayer, a friend's encouragement, or a middle-of-the-night whisper, I know now: God speaks to those who are listening.

I hear Him best in the quiet. In the morning. In nature. In moments when I'm not trying to control the outcome, but simply willing to be led. And I've learned that His voice often comes before His strategy. He doesn't give me the whole blueprint. He gives me a word. A name. A phrase. And waits to see if I'll trust Him with just that.

I do now. Because I've seen what happens when I do. Lives change. Assignments are birthed. And my own heart stays in tune with the One voice that never leads me astray. And every time I follow, I walk a little more freely. I trust a little more deeply. And I live a little more liberated, guided not by fear, but by faith.

17

I'm Not For Everyone
(And That's Okay)

THERE was a time in my life when I wanted to be understood by everyone. I wanted people to get my heart, respect my growth, and celebrate my change. But I've learned—sometimes painfully—that growth often leads to separation. And not everyone who starts with you is called to finish with you.

God has pruned so many people from my life that I've lost count. Some relationships ended in conflict, others in silence. Most didn't require a conversation; they simply dissolved as I changed. We were once connected by shared habits, shared trauma, or shared dysfunction. Overindulgence. Long nights of drinking. Parties that started fun but always left me feeling empty. It wasn't all evil, but it wasn't good either. And when I began choosing different values, priorities, rhythms, some people disappeared on their own. They weren't rejecting me; they just no longer recognized the version of me God was building.

But not every ending came quietly. There were moments when God asked me to walk away clearly and without apology. Business opportunities that had the right branding but the wrong spirit. People who used God's name while manipulating others for gain. Projects that looked holy on the outside but were spiritually toxic on the inside. In those moments, I had to say it aloud: "This is no longer for me."

At first, I struggled. I wondered if I was being judgmental. I feared rejection. I questioned whether I was overreacting. But God kept reminding me: obedience doesn't always make you popular. And discernment doesn't always make you comfortable. Sometimes, doing what's right with God means no longer fitting in with people who once felt like home.

I used to believe that peace came from keeping the circle intact. Now I know peace often comes from letting the circle change. I've stopped explaining my transformation. I've stopped shrinking to maintain connection. And

I've stopped confusing spiritual maturity with spiritual elitism. I'm not better than anyone; I'm just committed to walking in truth.

Living liberated means releasing the pressure to be chosen by everyone. It means trusting that God will align you with the right people for the season you're in. It means understanding that rejection isn't always a wound—sometimes it's a rescue. It means knowing that every time God removes something, He's making room for something greater.

Now, I walk away when peace is missing. I say no when the assignment feels forced. I bless people from a distance without needing to be invited to the table. And I rest on this truth: I'm not for everyone—and that's okay. I'm for the people God assigned me to. I'm for the path He placed me on. And I'm for the version of myself that is finally liberated enough to choose obedience over acceptance.

18

I Live Free, Whole, And Liberated

LIVING whole isn't a finish line; it's a way of being. It's not about perfection or having all the answers. It's about alignment, intimacy with God, and living every part of life with intention. I don't claim to have it all figured out. But what I do have now is peace. Rhythm. Clarity. And a relationship with God that leads every decision I make.

Wholeness looks like starting my day with God, with a posture of surrender, not only prayer. Before I reach for my phone, I reach for His presence. Before I scan my to-do list, I ask for His direction. It's not about checking spiritual boxes. It's about remembering who the Source is and refusing to move without Him.

I live in a rhythm of work and rest now. That means my work has a start time and an end time. I no longer grind until I break. I no longer wear exhaustion like a badge. I've learned that God blesses rhythm more than He blesses hustle. When I honor the sacredness of rest, I become a better leader, a better mother, a better woman.

I prioritize my temple (my body) because it's the house God gave me to steward. I move my body. I nourish it. I listen when it speaks. I don't push past pain to prove anything. Wholeness means honoring God with how I move, what I consume, and how I treat myself. It's not vanity, it's reverence.

I also explore what brings me joy. I say yes to creativity, to nature, to laughter, to rest. I try new things, take risks, and embrace adventure. I don't wait for perfect conditions to enjoy life. I walk in the abundance God promised. I used to think joy was a reward. Now I know—it's a spiritual practice. One that reminds me that liberation is not just freedom from something, but freedom into something: delight, peace, and presence.

But perhaps the most transformative part of living whole is how I receive love. God showed me I had to love

Him first. And I had to let Him love me back. That was the part I didn't know I was resisting. I thought serving was the same as intimacy. It's not. Love requires stillness. Vulnerability. Openness. And when I let God love me fully, deeply, without conditions, I stopped chasing love in places that couldn't hold me.

That's when I became free to love others. Not from emptiness, but from overflow. I no longer need people to complete me. I don't need platforms to validate me. I am rooted in God's love, and everything else flows from there.

There was a moment a few years ago that brought all of this into focus. My mother had come to live with me for a season, and eventually, she was ready to purchase a home again. She asked if I would move in with her. I didn't expect the emotions that surfaced—failure, fear, and regression. I prayed but still felt stuck between guilt and confusion.

I had to sit with why those emotions were so strong. In my experience as a Black woman in America, independence is a badge of success. We are taught to build our own, stand on our own, and never go backward. Generational living – especially when both generations are financially stable – is rarely modeled as a strength. It can look like struggle. It can feel like stagnation. And somewhere deep inside, I had absorbed the lie that moving into a home with my mother meant I had failed to build enough on my own.

It didn't matter that she had been living with me already. That was my house. This would be our house, and somehow, that subtle shift triggered something in me. It took my therapist asking gentle but direct questions to help me untangle it: Why is this a problem? What does this decision actually mean? Who told you this was regression?

My therapist's questions helped me to release my pride attached to independence. Working through this helped me to see this as a blessing. The truth was, I had never seen two financially stable Black women choose to live together as a strategy, not a necessity. I had to look beyond my cultural defaults to see how other communities leverage generational living to build wealth, create safety, and increase freedom. What I initially interpreted as failure was divine provision. What felt like going backward was God weaving our lives together for this season.

We bought the house and moved in together. My mother and I work well together. She is active. I am not alone. She is not alone. What I feared would shrink me has expanded my understanding of family, freedom, and favor.

Although my mom and I had moved in together, I still had a house to sell. I asked God for direction on whether I should sell it, rent it, or offer it as an Airbnb property.

Then I heard God whisper: "Call Michele."

We hadn't spoken in a while. I didn't have a plan. I was acting in obedience. During our conversation, Michele shared that she had been looking for a new home. As she described it, I realized it was the exact layout of the house I was preparing to leave. That single call—one whisper followed—opened the door for provision, peace, and clarity. My mother got the home she needed. I transitioned with grace. And once again, God confirmed: He cares about every detail.

Living whole means trusting the whispers. Trusting that God is orchestrating alignment even when we don't have the full picture. I don't just look for God in crisis—I listen for Him in transitions, in emotions, in relationships. The same God who gives me vision for business meets me in conversations about home and family. Nothing is too small for His concern.

Living whole doesn't mean life without challenges. It means I no longer live fragmented. No more pretending. No more over-functioning. No more compromising who I am to be accepted. I live as a woman who is clear, called, and committed to walking with God—daily.

This is my wholeness.

God first.

Rhythm honored.

Joy embraced.

Love received.

Peace protected.

Alignment is evident in every room I walk into.

It's not flashy. But it's sacred. It's steady. And it's real. And now, I offer it to you—not as a formula, but as an invitation.

Come live whole.

Come live free.

Come live liberated.

It's worth it.

About Me

Syrena N. Williams

I am first and foremost a child of God, and someone who believes deeply in the power and responsibility of relationships. I am a mother, daughter, sister, cousin, and a true friend. This is how I move through the world. I value presence, honesty, compassion, and the quiet work of truly knowing and caring for the people in my life. I am drawn to relationships that are meaningful and rooted in genuine care.

Like many people, I grew up surrounded by expectations, opinions, and narratives about who I should be and how I should move through the world. Some of those voices attempted to shape how I presented myself, while others used words that quietly chipped away at my confidence and self-esteem. Over time, I began to believe many of those messages as my truth.

Through God's continual tugging, reflection, faith, and life experience, I began to recognize that those narratives did not define me. Instead, I continued becoming who God was transforming me into.

One of the prayers that continues to shape my life is God allow me to see You in myself and in the people around me. When I approach others through that lens, everything shifts. It invites me to look beyond labels, assumptions, and past narratives and to recognize people as God sees them.

I understand that part of my role in the lives of others is simply to serve as a mirror, helping them recognize themselves as wonderfully made.

For many years, my work has involved walking alongside individuals and organizations as they learn, grow, and build meaningful lives and work. Along the way, my professional roles have included serving as an attorney, business consultant, coach, and educator. As my perspective deepened, the way I engaged my work began to change. Walking alongside people moved from being a task to becoming an honor. Development became less about solutions and more about caring for the whole person. Those relationships often grow into thought partnerships, building sessions, and, at times, discipleship.

Today, much of my work centers around an invitation I extend to others: to live liberated. Living Liberated encourages us to pause and examine the narratives that shape how we see ourselves, what we believe about our worth, and how we move through the world. It is an invitation to release what no longer aligns with truth and to embrace the person God is continually forming us to be.

Through my writing, speaking, and conversations with others, I invite people into the process of reflection and renewal. My book *Living Liberated: Letting Go of the Lies, Labels, and Longing to Be Free,* alongside its devotional companion, creates space for readers to wrestle honestly with their stories while rediscovering identity, freedom, and faith.

When I am not writing, speaking, or journeying with others, you can find me cooking, at the beach, dancing, laughing, and sharing meaningful conversations. There is nothing I enjoy more than building community and creating spaces where people can gather, be themselves, and encourage one another along the way.

Let's Connect